THE ORIGN AND THE GLORIOUS PAST OF THE ANDHRAS

THE ORIGN AND THE GLORIOUS PAST OF THE ANDHRAS

(A HISTORICAL SKETCH)

REV. J. M. ANTHOS

GYAN

Published by

Gyan Publishing House
5, Ansari Road
Daryaganj, New Delhi-110002
Phone: 011-47034999, 9811692060
E-mail: books@gyanbooks.com

Distribution Network
gyanbooks.com
India, USA, Canada, UK, Australia, France

ISBN : 978-81-212-3859-5 (PB)
First Published, 1925

2nd Impression 2020

Printed at: Gyan Press, Delhi.

The
Orign and the Glorious Past of the Andhras
Author: Rev. J. M. Anthos

To

The Most Rev. J. Aelen, D.D.,

Archbishop of Madras

The Writer

humbly dedicates

the following pages.

Shall Andhras' fame be left e'er veiled ?
To rend thy veil, so dark and soiled
O Andhra land, none, none so kind ?
Yet thy fame must dwell in e'ry mind.

J. M. A

FOREWORD

BY

The Hon. Sir A. P. PATRO,

Minister for Education, Government of Madras.

The Reverend Father J. Anthos requested me to read through the manuscript of his essay on the origin of the Andhras. The essay begins with the sources of study and describes the migration of Aryans and non-Aryans into Jambudvipa. The learned author defines the Dasyus of Rigveda, the Kolaryans and Dravidians who latterly occupied the Southern parts of India. The term Andhra appears in the hymns of Rigveda and the Andhras are described as a race of mixed origin. The author relies on the researches of Mr. Vincent Smith and bases his conclusions on an inscription recorded in 144 A.D. by the Queen Mother Andhra Bala Sari. The Andhras during that period are said to have destroyed the Sakas, Yavanas and Pallavas. I cannot pretend to have analysed the interesting sketch of the Andhras in this paper, but there is no doubt whatever that the learned author has investigated the problem before him with great care. There is no doubt that this contribution, introductory as it is, will add an important chapter to the history of the Andhras. The Andhras will be grateful for such valuable contribution to their history.

PANTHEON GARDEN,
EGMORE, MADRAS,
8th April, 1924.

A. P. PATRO.

PREFACE.

While yet a student in the Theological Seminary at Kandy, I desired, being an Andhra myself, to read a paper at the Literary Academy on the history of the Andhra people. For this purpose I searched the magnificent library of the institution, which has a good stock of books on a variety of subjects and in different languages. This library is rich in oriental literature, chiefly on historical subjects. Despite all these advantages I could not collect sufficient material for my small paper for the simple reason that there was no book available on the past history of the Telugu people. But I was not discouraged. As I began to reflect on the subject, I could not help thinking that as the Andhras were scattered over a large tract of land known as Thrilingana, or Andhra Desa, now numbering over twenty millions, or one-fifteenth of the teeming millions of India's population, they could not be without any history. They could not have come into existence all of a sudden, they must have had their origin, sometime in the dim past. On these considerations, I had recourse to every book available on Indian History wherein fragments of the origin and growth of the Telugu people were given. I also tried to get as much information as possible from Pandits and other Scholars versed in ancient history of India. Then I drew my own conclusions. In the difficult task of collecting materials for a connected narrative, I often thought of giving up the work as a trying and difficult job. Even after completing my brief narrative, I had no desire to publish it. But eminent men who kindly went through the manuscript encouraged me and urged me to publish it. In the first place my special thanks are due to Mr. A. P. C. Albuquerque, the Deputy Official Assignee, High Court, Madras, for the valuable help rendered. I am very grateful to the Hon'ble Sir A. P. Patro, Minister for Education, for reading my booklet and for introducing it to the public with a kind foreword, especially at a time when his time was fully occupied with the Budget discussion in the Madras Legislative Council. I am also very thankful to many kind gentlemen, to mention only a few the Hon'ble Mr. Justice Ramesam Pantulu, Judge, High Court, Madras, Mr. Selvaraj Reddiar, B.A., L.T., Mr. J. Franco, M.A., Ag. Personal Assistant to the Director of Public Instruction, Mr. Glyn Barlow, M.A., formerly editor of "Madras Times," Mr. J. A. Saldhana, B.A., LL.B., M.L.C., and Mr. Rathnaswamy, M.A., (Cantab), Bar-at-law. M.L.C., the

Principal, Pachayappa's College, Madras, who expressed their appreciation of my modest effort in writing this brief history of the Telugu people entitled "The Origin and the Glorious Past of the Andhras."

PERAMBUR,
Easter, 1925

J. M. A.

CONTENTS.

THE
ORIGIN AND THE GLORIOUS PAST OF THE ANDHRAS.

To rend thy veil, so dark and soiled
O Andhra land, none, none so kind?

INTRODUCTION.

The wonderful history of the rise and fall of once mighty nations is one to which we are not strangers. We know how nation after nation, city after city, rose to opulence and power, and in time sank into insignificance and decay.

To take but a few examples, on the banks of the Nile an ancient civilization was evolved and nurtured and its secret now lies buried amid the tombs and monuments, beneath the desert sands.

Fifteen hundred years before the advent of Christ, its merchants bought from India, her muslins and silks, her spices and pearls, of more value than gold. The ships of the Assyrians and Babylonians sailed forth in all their glory and splendour to buy from India the teakwood, wherewith the people of Ur built their palaces and the gold of the East, with which they adorned their maidens and guilded their temples.

Again Tyre, the City of the Phœnicians, grew in the days of

Hiram, to be the mistress of the Seas and the merchant of the people of many isles.

When Solomon received a mandate from his father, David, to build the temple of Jehovah, it was from Tyre that he summoned wise men to bring gold and ivory, sandalwood and silver from the East.

But now how many are there to think of the Egyptians, the Assyrians, the Babylonians and the Phœnicians? The fame of these once mighty nations is buried deep in the Eastern deserts.

So too with greater truth can one say of India, and in particular of Andhra India, whose glory was washed away by the tides of time, though she acquired this glory amid her pomp and splendour, first satiating the needs of her own sons and then those of many a mighty nation.

The story of this noble land then and in particular of Andhra Desa and its people, the Andhras, and their past achievements, we shall endeavour to narrate in these few pages.

As we shall soon show, the Andhras were the pride of India and their deeds and achievements were her glory. To write of Andhra Desa is to write a good and select portion of the History of India.

SOURCES OF STUDY.

Before we proceed to make a detailed study of the subject, we shall give a few particulars about the sources, from which materials can be drawn for our study. It has been said that a characteristic of the ancient Hindu mind was to speculate, instead of to investigate. The old Indian Geographer did not travel, explore or survey, but sat down and dreamt of a central mountain of a height greater than that of the sun, moon and the stars and of circular oceans of curds and clarified butter. Similarly the ancient Hindu historian did not examine documents, coins and monuments, investigate historical facts, weigh evidences, balance probabilities, scatter the chaff to the winds and gather the grain of truth, in his granary. Hence arises the difficulty of writing a complete and authentic history of India. Even in our times we find historians who, in spite of the vast resources at their disposal, betray their spirit of speculation in their writings. Nations, like individuals, have their merits and defects.

The Indian mind has been at work for over 3,000 years and has produced a vast literature, chiefly in Sanskrit. In some respects India took the lead, for there were only two nations in the whole history of the world, namely, the

Hindus and the Greeks who have conceived, independently and without any suggestions from others, the two sciences of Logic and Grammar. In Mathematics the Indians have the glory of inventing the decimal notation, without which the Greeks and Romans were at a great disadvantage. Again, for centuries, the Hindus were in vain trying to invent an elixir, which would render men immortal. They also falsely believed in the occult powers supposed to be acquired by "Yoga" which would enable them to get at the knowledge of the past and the future, of hidden treasures and mines.

PHILOLOGY AND ARCHÆOLOGY.

However, there exist to-day, an elixir to immortalize the dead and a "Yogasastra" to reveal the knowledge of the past, and of the hidden treasures, invented by the practical yogis, the present day philologists and archæologists. The dead restored to life and the hidden treasures brought to light by these Yogis are too numerous to be mentioned here. The Indian kings who have been forgotten for centuries are brought to life and are made to live for ever in the pages of history. It is this elixir of philology and this yoga of archæology, which provide us with materials for our subject.

Though much has been done in this line, a great deal more has still to be done. For there are some centuries in the history of India which may be called the "Dark Ages." We may cite, as a glaring instance of this kind, the third of our Era, which is one of the darkest spaces in the spectrum of Indian History. Almost every event of that period is concealed from view by an impenetrable veil of oblivion. Great praise is due therefore to oriental scholars, who by their unsparing pains manage to unearth historical facts from the mines of obscurity; so that like other sections of Indian History, the History of the Andhras also may regain its lustre.

THE FRUITFUL LABOURS OF SCHOLARS.

That this is being done to our history is seen from the words of Mr. Vincent Smith, a great authority on Indian History who says that the most important and powerful of the last seven kings of the Andhra dynasty is Yajnasri who reigned for the space of 29 years. His rare silver coins, says the same author, certainly prove a renewal of relation with the western Satraps and probably point to his unrecorded conquests. The coins of this king's time, bearing the figure of a ship, suggest the inference that his power was not confined to land alone. The future of research work is full of hopes, and the labours of scholars are bound to be fruitful. For at the recent survey conducted at Amaravati, once the capital of the Andhras, they have unearthed a number of sculptured figures, inscriptions, pottery and rare coins, which are sure to throw further light on the forgotten history of the Andhras.

MODERN ANDHRA DESA.

A word in this connection about the present location of the Andhras, and also about the origin of the word "India", will not, we think, be out of place. The Telugu people at present occupy, roughly speaking, that part of India which may be described as a semicircle, of which, the centre is Rajahmundry on the river Godavari and on the North-Eastern Railway line, the distance between the said town and the City of Madras, taken as radius. The area of the Andhra land, known in history as "Thrilingana," or "Andhra Desa," is over a hundred thousand square miles or nearly twice the area of England. Its inhabitants now number roughly over twenty millions. Thus giving us to understand that there is one Andhra in every fifteen of the teeming millions of Hindustan.

ORIGIN OF THE WORD "INDIA".

The name "India" is derived from the Greek and Roman adaptations of the word "Shindu," Hindu a term used by the Persians to designate their Aryan brethren, because the latter had settled in the "Shindu" (Sindu, Hindu, Indu) or the "Septashindava" the land of the seven rivers, namely, the River Indus, with its five tributaries and the River Sarasvati. According to Herodotus the Greeks knew this name from the Persians. It should be noted that "Sindu," India, was originally occupied by non-Aryans and then conquered (partially) by the Aryans, who after their occupation began to be called "Shindoi" Sindoi, Hindoi, Indoi, Hindus, by the Greeks through their Persian brethren.

THE DATE OF THE FIRST MIGRATION OF THE ARYANS.

We shall now try to establish the probable date of the original inhabitation of India, before we begin to consider, who were its first inhabitants and whence they migrated into this country. To find out the probable date of the first migration, the only source available is the Rigveda, which forms the greatest literary monument of the early Aryan settlements in the Punjab.

Hindus believe the Rigveda to be "before all time." Some scholars say that there are evidences to corroborate the statement, that Aryan settlements in India were going on as early as 3000 B.C., nearly 5,000 years ago. But what some scholars have inferred from astronomical dates that the computation of the Rigveda took place about 1400 B.C. is abundantly established. Professor Hunter, probably the greatest authority on Indian antiquities, thinks that there is nothing shocking to probability in supposing that the Hindu dynasties and their ramifications have spread through an interval about 12 centuries anterior to the great war of the Mahabarata, an event which he is disposed to ascribe to about the 14th century before Christ.

From this, we may say that the regal dynasties of Hindustan began to exist about two thousand six hundred years before our era. But according to other scholars like Monier Williams and Monsignor Laounan, the Aryans were colonizing the Punjab between 2000 and 1500 B.C. Taking the minimum date then, we may safely conclude that the Aryans were in India at least before 1500 B.C. All scholars agree that the different non-Aryan tribes settled in India, long before the Aryans. But they have hitherto attached very little importance to this occurrence. It is our duty to establish the probable date of the non-Aryan migration.

THE DATE OF THE MIGRATION OF THE NON-ARYANS.

The great king Sesostres, known in history as Rameses II, as narrated by the historian called the Sicilian, sent forth even before the days of Moses "a navy of 400 sail into the Red Sea, conquered all Asia, passed over the River Ganges and likewise pierced through all India to the main ocean."

Diodorus tells us how, 2,000 years before Christ, the famous Queen

Semiramis carried over land a fleet of 2,000 boats to the Indus, which she crossed at the head of three million foot soldiers and 2,000 horsemen and then fought the Emperor Stabrobates, only to fall back defeated and herself wounded.

If this event be true at least to some extent, what a powerful non-Aryan nation or nations must have dwelt on the banks of the Indus, to overcome or even to resist such a large and mighty army! From this we can easily imagine the period at which the non-Aryan tribes must have settled on the banks of the Indus, or thereabouts, so as to form such a powerful nation about 2000 B.C.

According to this computation we can establish the period, when the original inhabitation of India took place, to be somewhere between 3500 and 3000 B.C. Anyhow we may be sure that this took place at least before 2000 B.C., and not after. After this who were the first inhabitants of India and whence had they emigrated are the two great problems to be solved.

THE FIRST INHABITANTS OF INDIA.

Sir William Hunter correctly remarks that " India forms a great museum of races, in which we can study man from his lowest to his highest stage of culture." Indeed though shut in on all sides by great mountain ranges or by broad seas, India's surpassing fertility and wealth attracted outside peoples to such an extent that there are found in this country racial types, languages and dialects in various stages of development and progress, which will bewilder the cleverest of ethnologists. Thus in accordance with the ethnological results obtained so far the races that have contributed to make up the population of India are of Turanian and Aryan origin.

This we learn also from the same author, who says that our earliest glimpses of Hindustan disclose two races, struggling for the soil.

As the Aryans come in only as a side issue and play a secondary part in the subject under treatment, we need hardly devote our time to a lengthy consideration of that race and its origin. Suffice it to say that they came to India long after the Turanians and that the two races were engaged in a deadly struggle for the mastery of the soil. Taking then the Turanians, we should at the outset mention that this race takes its name from the word "Turan" meaning the land of darkness. "Under this term," says a German Historian, "we comprise all the nations that are neither Aryan nor Semitic, whether they descended from a common stock or not". As the first settlers of Europe go by the name of Turanian, so also, all the tribes that inhabited this vast country, before the Aryan advent, were familiar to philologists, even until very recently, only by the same word "Turan" or the land of darkness.

DO ALL NON-ARYANS BELONG TO ONE AND THE SAME STOCK?

At this stage, it is our duty to examine whether all the tribes, who came to India before the Aryan migration, belonged to one and the same stock. The oldest hymns of the Rigveda give us a clue to this difficult and intricate problem and say that the greater part of India was then covered with dense forests, with scattered villages and towns, occupied by the earliest settlers, who were of a dark complexion and spoke a strange language. The same hymns further declare that the Aryans had racial pride to an extravagant degree, showing contempt for and hatred of the other nations or tribes, with whom they had come in contact. The new comers from the cold regions prided themselves on their fair complexion and contemptuously called the earlier inhabitants, black skinned, foresters, goblins, and demons. This contempt and hatred was due to colour distinction and, according to the Vedas, to the stout resistance offered by the latter to the Aryans.

There is nothing to be wondered at in this fact, for, as we all know, the same thing happens even in our own times. It is from this colour distinction that some of the Indian languages acquired a beautiful and polite expression for ascertaining one's caste, *i.e.*, "(meevarna-memi)", meaning what is your colour, but now used as a very polite term for ascertaining one's caste.

THE DASYUS OF THE RIGVEDA.

The old inhabitants of India were known to the intruding Aryans as "Dasyus," a term which at that time meant simply foreign people or strangers. Years rolled on, then there came a time when the borders of North-Western India could no longer contain the intruders. Like all other invaders, the proud Aryans could acquire territories only by an appeal to arms, so that the Dasyus of old had now become their enemies, which was the second meaning of the word "Dasyus"; finally those that were conquered were addressed as "Dasyus", with the third meaning slaves.

FINNS AND LAPPS.

In Europe the Aryans, known also as Indo-Europeans, displaced the early inhabitants, the Finns and the Lapps of Turanian origin, driving them to the farthest north. But in India, on the other hand, their Aryan brethern made no doubt a similar attempt, but only with partial success. This we learn from their own hymns, which also speak of the enormous wealth of the original inhabitants.

THE ENORMOUS WEALTH AND HIGH CIVILIZATION OF NON-ARYANS.

> " Subdue the might of the Dasa
> May we, through Indra divide his collected wealth ".

The same hymns bear witness also to the power and civilization of the Dasyus, for we learn from the following hymns of the " Vedas " that they possessed forts and cities :—

> "Indra and Agni, by one effort together
> Ye have shattered 90 forts belonging to the Dasyus."
>
> "O Indra impetuous thou didst
> Shatter by thy bolt 99 cities for Puru."

One or two facts may be inferred from the foregoing. Some of the Dasyus were conquered and made slaves, or, abandoning their cities and fortresses, had taken shelter somewhere else.

Further assuming that the Aryans had some kind of civilization at this time, we may affirm that the people, with whom they came in contact, also possessed the same, if not a superior kind of civilization.

If not, the Aryans would not have prayed to their Gods to destroy the formidable forts and hand over to them the beautiful cities and vast riches of the Dasyus.

The Aryans following the good old maxim,

> "the simple plan that they should take,
> who have the power and they should keep, who can."

during their advance into India, gradually established themselves in the forests, fields, towns and villages of the original inhabitants who fought as bravely as they could against the invaders.

The war of invasion lasted for centuries, perhaps for milleniums, nor were the non-Aryan tribes completely subdued at any period.

PRIMITIVE SAVAGES.

In the pre-historic age there lived in India bands of wild savages, who were in the habit of wandering along the river banks in search of food. This fact is gleaned from the chipped flint or quartzite arrow heads, chisels, and axes, which are dug up to-day in the alluvial deposits of the great Indian river valleys. It is to these people, who as worshippers of their ancestors' spirits used to bury their dead with great veneration, that the "Dolmans," which are found in great numbers over hills and hilly tracts and in the woods, which give no easy access to civilized man, are attributed. These graves when opened were known to contain bones of ordinary human size, together with paleolithic implements and occasionally Roman coins of the first century. From this it is clear that some of these people lived in the times of our own era. Further we understand that the same type of people must have been gradually driven by the invading races to the lofty mountain ranges, where, amid the dense forests, their descendants still live undisturbed, retaining all their primitive simplicity, superstition, belief and habits.

In the light of the statements, above referred to, one may reasonably conclude that all the different tribes of this country who are classed as "Turanian" are not of one and the same stock.

KOLARIANS AND DRAVIDIANS.

A careful ethnological examination of the various non-Aryan languages of India shows that the primitive people of India belonged to the three great distinct stocks, known as the Tibeto-Burman, the Kolarian and the Dravidian.

The Kolarians to whom the term "Turanian" should strictly speaking be applied, as we shall presently show, and who migrating from Central Asia and the steppes of Tartary and Tibet through the North-Eastern passes forced their way into India by successive incursions, are believed to be the most ancient people that had settled in this country. They are represented at present by the Santals and the Kols, with their oval faces and flat noses. We must be careful, says Monier Williams, not to confound the great Dravidian races with the uncivilized aboriginal tribes of India. The Dravidian races, continues the same author, probably symbolized by the Ravanas and Vibishanas of the Ramayana, were the precursors of the Sanskrit speaking Aryans and probably had their origin, like the Aryans, in the same districts of Central Asia, whence they immigrated, by the same mountain passes into the Punjab and Northern India, and he further opines that they were partially amalgamated with the advancing Aryans, though they were mostly driven southwards.

On the other hand, affirms the same author, those who were symbolized by the monkey armies of Hanuman were the Santals, the Bills and the Kols.

For our purpose it is quite enough that from this we are in a position to differentiate between the Aborigines and the other early tribes, whose occupation of India preceded that of the Aryans.

CONFLICTING VIEWS.

But Doctor Caldwell, who is probably the greatest authority on Tamil literature, in his "Comparative Grammar" of the Dravidian languages, after discussing with great ability the affiliation of this family, concludes that they were the very first inhabitants of India and that they were driven southwards by other invaders, who in turn, were subdued by the Aryans.

This view is in conflict with that of Monier Williams. However, we should not suppose that all the Dravidians had entered India at one and the same time and, so to say, formed one single group, tribe, or nation though their advent into this country preceded that of the Aryans. From what we have seen already it is clear that there were two distinct non-Aryan races in India, excluding of course the third race, known as the Tibeto-Burman, which, for brevity sake, we will simply pass over by saying that these people entered India through the North-eastern passes like the Kolarians. The term Kolarian is applied to the people who were in India before the Aryans and with whom the latter came in contact. It was about them that the Vedic hymns abounded in scornful epithets and according to Dr. Caldwell it is those people that the Dravidians had to face in battle and abandoning their homes in the north, were forced to take shelter in the south.

The whole tribe takes the name "Kolarian" from the term "Kol," which is the name of a division of the same race, in other words, the name of a part applies to the whole race. It is only recently that this term has been adopted by Mr. Campbell for the entire tribe. Thus it is clear that the people who were in India before the Aryan advent were the Tibeto-Burmans, the Kolarians including Kols, the Santals, the Bills and also other minor tribes, all of them classified as "Turanians" and "Dravidians." As we have said, there are contrary opinions on this subject, some saying that the

Dravidians came in contact with the Aryans, and others that they were opposed by the Kolarians.

DRAVIDIANS RESIST ARYANS.

But whatever may be the opinions held by scholars, one thing is agreed upon, that the Dravidians were forced to go from the north to their present home in the south and that all the people who are now conveniently classed as Dravidians did not enter India all at the same time. We have seen already that the enemies of the Aryans possessed strong forts, beautiful cities and immense wealth, which the latte[illegible] und it very difficult to captur[illegible] pposing we exclude the Dravidians, who among the insignificant Kolarian or Turanian Tribes could have been so powerful and possessed such strong forts and beautiful cities as to excite the admiration of the Aryans? By this process of elimination, we can safely arrive at the conclusion that the Andhro-Dravidians were the people, who resisted the Aryans and over whom the Aryans had only partial success. Some of them as we have already pointed out were defeated and took shelter elsewhere, while others bravely defended themselves and proved a terror to the Aryans. Who were then the people that stood their ground and would not abandon their homes? A glance at the ancient history of our country will give an answer to this question. We know the part played by the Andhras in the early times and this should go to prove that the Andhras were the people, who could not be defeated by the Aryans and that, if they were not the only people that resisted the Aryans, they certainly formed a good part of the whole race that did not experience the misfortune of abandoning their homes and cities. We have sufficient reasons to show that the Andhras, in the early times when the Aryans first entered the regions of the Punjab, were the people who fought the invaders and could not be driven southwards.

THE TERM "ANDHRA."

The very name of the tribe "Andhra" is in itself a proof. "An" meaning "not" and "dra" from the root "dru" in Sanskrit, meaning to run (अः not द द्रा) signifies to run or to run away. Thus the word "Andra" would mean, not driven, could not be driven or withstood and consequently resisted. It will be also interesting to note that, in many languages, both in oriental and occidental, the root dru (dra) has the same meaning, *viz.*, to run, *e.g.*, Telugu తరుము దరుము tharumu, dharumu, to drive, Sanskrit, "dru" to put to flight, Tamil துரத்து (Dhurathu) to drive, English "Drive," Greek "Dremos" to drive or that which runs, Anglo-Saxon "drifan," Dutch "Drijven" and German "Triben."

We are also familiar with the fact, that the earliest non-Aryan kingdoms in India were the three southern kingdoms of the Tamils and the two Telugu kingdoms of "Andhra" and "Kalinga." As to the importance of the "Andhra" kingdom, let us hear what the eminent historian, Mr. Vincent Smith, has to say. "In the days of Chandra Gupta and Magasthenes, the Greek Ambassador at the Court of the abovesaid king in the year 300 B.C., the Andhra nation, probably a Dravidian people, now represented by a large population speaking the Telugu language, was reputed to possess a military force second only to that at the command of King Prasii Chandra Gupta Mauriya." History tells us that at this time the abovenamed Aryan prince was the first in power in the whole of India and it is enough for us to know that the Andhra kingdom was the second in the whole of India, as early as 300 B.C. We may add in passing that this term "Andhra," both in Telugu and Tamil, has the meaning of mysterious, wonderful, invincible and terrible. As to the antiquity of the term "Andhra" we may point out here that it was in existence as early as in the days of Aiterea-Bramana of the Rigveda. As all those who resisted the

Aryans were called demons or Pisaichas, the Andhras also are represented therein as wild and terrible and as demons, thus showing that they really proved a terror to the Aryans. The Vedas themselves declare that the Andhras as a tribe were known to the early Aryans and that in the south of India, though inhabited, in the vedic times the people were not formed in large tribes, nor were they known by any common name at this time, except by the term barbarian.

ARYANS ADDRESS ANDHRAS AS DEMONS.

There is nothing strange in the fact, that the Aryans addressed the people who resisted and proved a terror to them, as demons or Pisaichas; for to the old Chinese the European nations were foreign devils, and to the ancient Greeks and Romans all nations that had no intercourse with them were barbarians. Likewise the Indian Astronomer Garga, who wrote in the first century before Christ, said that the Greeks were "very barbarians."

Moreover "Pisachi" was the name applied to the language of the terrible Andhras at the time of the Rigveda. However it is rather strange that the language of these people known now and acknowledged as the "most musical," "or the sweet Italian of the East," should have been styled by the Aryans of old, as Pisachi, or the language of the devils.

The fact that in the first century A.D., a book in the Pisachi tongue entitled "Brihat Katha", or the great story book, was written by the minister of the Andhra king Hala, himself a great literary man, is a proof that the language of the Andhras was continued to be known by the same appellation "Pisachi" even in our own era.

Thus, summing up, we may say that the Andhra nation was in existence during the early Vedic times, that they took a prominent part in the task of checking the Aryans and that they did not lose their territory like others, but grew up to be a powerful nation, second only to the kingdom of Magada in 300 B.C.; while Kalinga also an independent Andhra kingdom which separated itself from the main Andhra Empire, was also in existence, possessing 60,000 infantry, 1,000 cavalry and 700 war elephants. We may as well add here that the three Tamil kingdoms of Chera, Chola and Pandia were also existing at this time.

However the Andhra nation with its singular origin and independent growth was by a gross mistake, as we will show presently, called Dravidian by the early missionaries of this country. It is only on this account that the

Andhras are classed as the Dravidas, a term which applies, strictly speaking, to the Tamils and the Malayalees. We must say that this classification is most improper, because, in view of the facts stated above, the Andhras had such a singular origin and independent growth.

THE TERM "DRAVIDIAN" WRONGLY APPLIED TO THE ANDHRAS.

There are historians who believe that the Aryans began their intercourse with the people in the south, only about 500 B.C. It was owing to this intercourse that the Aryans called the people of the south "Dravidians" or Dravidas.

The word Dravida is mentioned in the book of Manu (X. 44) in the division of the people, where its author shows that the Dravidians were not included among the four castes. Whatever may be the date of the compilation of the "Manava Dharmasastra," there is no difficulty in admitting that it is posterior to the Vedic times. If the assertion of Dr. Caldwell be true that the Dravidians were the first to come to India and that they were defeated not by the Aryans but by the Kolarians and were forced to go to the south, it will not be difficult to admit the statement, chiefly of Mr. Vincent Smith, that the Aryans had not come in contact with the people of the south before about 500 B.C. All the same we hear the people of the south were known to the Aryans at this time by the term "Dravidian."

But it is difficult to assert that the land they occupied was also called "Dravida" by the Aryans. On the other hand South India was known to the Aryans at the time of Manu only as "Malekadesa." In fact before the middle of the 7th century A.D. no definite mention was made about the word "Dravida."

It was only during the reign of Narasimha Varman I the Pallava King that the Chinese traveller, Hiouen Tsang, who visited

" Kanchi " or the modern Conjeevaram in the year 640 A.D. and stayed there for a considerable time, called the kingdom of which Kanchi was the capital by the name " Dravida " and described it as about 1,000 miles in circuit.

THE CHOLA KINGDOM RULED BY THE "PALLAVAS."

This was evidently the Chola kingdom of the south and consequently the other southern kingdoms Chera, Pandia and Kerala were not included in this. The Chola kingdom was conquered by the Pallavas who were a new class of people not of Indian origin. They invaded the Andhra Desa but were driven south by the Andhra King "Villivayakura" II, who ruled from 113 to 138 A.D. From the following it is clear that the Pallavas were already a ruling race in the south. Their king Sivaskandavarman was lord of so many subordinate chiefs that he considered himself fit to perform the "Aswameda" horse sacrifice, a rite permissible only to a paramount sovereign. The Chinese traveller mentioned above calls this kingdom of the Pallavas "Dravida", for which reasons we cannot definitely say. It is because the land was occupied by the Pallavas that were driven by the Andhras or because it was occupied by the Cholas, whose forefathers were driven towards the south by the Aryans or the Kolarians as the case may be. Whatever may be the truth, one thing is certain, the two kingdoms "Andhra" and "Dravida", the former a Telugu and the latter a Tamil, were quite separate and independent kingdoms. The reader, who is familiar with the origin of the Andhras, their growth of power and their existence already at the time of the Vedas, will see no reason for mixing up "Dravida" with "Andhra" or including the Andhras among the Dravidas.

CAUSE OF THE MISTAKE EXPLAINED.

But why are the Tamils and the Telugu people classed as "Dravidian"? Until the middle of the 19th century, the various languages of our country were known only by their own respective names and were not classified under any philological group. The languages of India, excepting the Aryan, were, as we have already stated, known only by the term "Turanian." The philologists after a careful examination and study divided the languages of India into four distinct classes or groups and named them as Tibeto-Burman, Kolarian, Dravidian and Aryan. At this time the language of the Andhras was wrongly considered as of Aryan origin, owing to its admixture with Sanskrit and its dialects and in time, when the mistake was found out, it was conveniently shoved into the Dravidian group. Certainly among all the cognate languages which have been grouped together and named as Dravidian, the farthest removed from each other are Tamil and Telugu and not one entire sentence in one language is intelligible to those who are acquainted only with the other. However, one should not find it difficult to admit that there is some relation and connection between the two languages and they are on closer examination found to be such, for they contain many words, which, though very much disguised and mutilated, are identically the same at root. It is on this account that Monier Williams is of opinion that the people speaking Tamil, Telugu, Kanarese and Malayalam, etc., had their origin, like the Aryans, in the same districts of Central Asia, whence they emigrated by the same mountain passes into the Punjab and Northern India. If we give credit to this statement, we can conclude that though the Dravidians had entered India all at once, the fore-fathers of the Tamils and the Malayalees got themselves separated from the Andhras and took shelter in the south. Or if the statement of Bishop Caldwell is to be followed, we should say that the people who speak the 12 cognate languages of the south made their way into the Punjab, before the Aryans, not at the same time, but at different times and by different tribes or groups.

Further we may conclude that the Tamils were the first to enter the Hindustan, only to make way for the other non-Aryans, now known as the Kolarians, and that the Andhras were the tribe that came into this country later on and faced the Aryans, together with the Kolarians, when they invaded India. The connection between the two languages Andhra and Dravida is understood from the fact that they had the same cradle in Central Asia. Whether they separated themselves within or without the limits of "Jambu-dvipa," we cannot definitely say. But it is evident that the people now known as Tamils were together once with the Telugus in potentia. Evidently, of the tribes that resisted the Aryans, some were conquered and made slaves, while the others that could not be subdued were in India, side by side with the Aryans, as distinct and powerful clans and even known by their own respective names. But what became of these tribes, and how were they considered and treated by the Aryans, are questions that need elucidation now.

MINGLING OF CASTES.

To answer this, we should bear in mind that during the vedic period caste rules were not so rigorous as in the days of "Manu." It is believed that under such circumstances people could shift from one caste to another. The hymns of the Rigveda show that the Aryan tribes, as well as their allies the non-Aryans such as the "Gandharas" and the "Bharatas", were engaged in a fearful civil war. We find a confederacy of ten tribes, including the non-Aryan, (ignoble), Bharatas, formed under the leadership of King "Kutra", against the Aryan tribe "Tristu" and the rishi "Visvamitra" is said to have taken the sides of the ten tribes mentioned above. Visvamitra himself, be it noted, was not originally a Brahman, but obtained that rank by super-human feats of asceticism.

The same rishi praises in his hymns of the "Rigveda" his non-Aryan allies and calls them wise. This is an instance of the adaptation of a non-Aryan tribe into the Aryan stock.

The Bharatas who were converted by Visvamitra became so thoroughly organised and incorporated and held such a prominent position among the Aryans, that in after days the land of the Bharatas or Bharatavarsa was the name applied to Aryan India.

NON-ARYAN TRIBES ADMITTED INTO THE ARYAN FAMILY.

Again the great Kshatria tribe of Kurus is one of the non-Aryan tribes of the Vedic times.

It is very significant that in the Rigveda we hear of one Krishna as a non-Aryan king and a loud, bellowing, marauding chief, whom "Indra" destroyed for the benefit of the Aryan nation. (R.V.V. VIII 96 13-15).

The Nishadas were Dasyus in the eyes of the Vedic Aryans, but Nala their king, described in the Mahabarata as a virtuous man, well versed in the Vedas, was a perfect Kshatria. This fact must be quite familiar to the readers of "Nala Charitra," a story narrated by the great sage Vyasa, in the "Aranyaparva," 15th chapter of Mahabarata, to the five brothers, known as the Pandavas. Nala is therein held up as a model of patient endurance and kingly virtues for the Pandava Princes to imitate and as such the story must bring home to our minds the mutual relations between the Aryans and the non-Aryans and the high esteem with which the latter were treated by the former. More examples may be cited to show how non-Aryan tribes were admitted into the Aryan family according to their division of society into Bhahmins, Kshatrias,

Vaisias and Sudras, as Priests, warriors, traders and servants.

THE ANDHRAS A RACE OF MIXED ORIGIN.

ARYO-ANDHRAS.

The result of this free intercourse between the Aryans and the non-Aryans was that after the Vedic period the people of Malva, Behar and the Dekkan were found to be generally of a mixed origin. In the same way the Andhras, who were despised by the Vedic Aryans, were treated as equals and inter-marriages took place to such an extent that the inhabitants of the whole country became a mixed race. Manu, the author of Manava-Darmasastra recognised the descendants of the non-Aryan chiefs, who married Aryan damsels as pure Kshatrias; the free intercourse of races by mixed marriages is expressly allowed by many writers of Sastras and raising the status of the male who married a girl of a lower caste, after some generations of progeny had passed, is also recognised. At the time when "Manu" codified his laws, southern India was mentioned in his book as the land of the "Milechas" or barbarians, where the four castes did not dwell.

But the Andhras were not included among the degraded tribes mentioned expressly in the "Manava-Darmasastra." Hence we cannot but conclude from this that at the time of Baudhayana 600 B.C. the Andhras were considered to be of mixed origin and later at the time of "Manu" they were on a footing of equality with the Aryans.

Dr. Bandarkar asserts on the authority of "Yajanavalkya" "our Aryan ancestors found no difficulty in fully mixing with the aboriginal tribes and even in contracting marriage with any but the most degraded classes." Many of the "Smritis" and "Sastras" permit connection of the twice born with the women of the lower castes, in addition to the most approved form of marriage. It is evident that the Telugu people were on equal footing with the Aryans and that they, more than others, adhered strictly to the caste rules, as the long inscription recorded in 144 A.D. by the Queen Mother, Andhra Balasari, would show. In it she glories as the Mother of the Hero who "destroyed the Sakas, Yavanas and the Pallavas and prevented the mixing of the four castes."

THE "PURANAS."

The "Puranas" will also bear witness to this fact. We should not forget that the Hindus have so great a veneration for these 18 books and consider them so sacred that, though none of them can claim a date earlier than the 3rd or 2nd century after Christ, they would speak of them as if they were "from all times", as the word "Puran," meaning "of old," would show. These self same puranas are the records of the deeds of the Andhra kings.

These books which are so much revered by all orthodox Hindus contain practically the entire history of the great Andhra Dynasty together with that of the Aryans. This certainly goes to prove the statement of the philologists that the language men speak is not necessarily a proof of the race to which they belong. It must not be thought that all who speak the Dravidian languages are of unmixed origin or that all who speak the various Aryan dialects are pure blooded Aryans. If this holds good to any nation, it should be so to the Andhras, for they held their sway over the Kingdom of "Magada," thus ruling the whole of the Aryan country, whose people, to use the words of queen "Balasari," bore the sweet Andhra yoke for quite a long period.

THE LANGUAGE OF THE ANDHRAS.

Now we may as well consider a while about the language of the Andhras in the early times known as the "Pisachi" tongue. As time went on, the Andhras spread and settled themselves over a large area in the Dekkan chiefly in the Northern parts of the modern Madras Presidency. This land was called "Trilingana" or "Trinaga" and hence their language took the name of Thenugu or Telugu.

These tracts of land, where the Andhras or the Telugu people dwell, contained three Hindu Temples built on three hills. The land is also called Telingana which is a corruption of Thrilingana or the country of the three lingams. From Thrilingana comes Telugu and from Thrinaga, Tenugu, meaning the language of the people, who inhabited the land in which there were either three lingams or three hills. The origin of this word is interesting. There were once three Hindu temples built on three hills, (nagam=hill), one at Kalahastri in Nellore District, another at Sriselem in Kurnool District and the third at Dhraksharanam in Godavari District. In each of these temples there was a lingam sacred to Siva; hence the name Thenugu or Telugu, as explained above.

Telugu the language of the Andhras is mixed with Sanskrit and chiefly with its dialects Marathi and Uria, so that, when the philologists divided the languages of this country into four main groups, they were at a loss to know under which group they should place this language. So they wrongly of course grouped it along with the Aryan dialects. Some orthodox Telugu pandits even now do not own that their language is not a dialect of Sanskrit. But a great majority of them do admit that it is "Vikruti" and we shall presently see what that word means.

THE "BASHA" OF "PANINI", THE FAMOUS GRAMMARIAN.

In the early Vedic times we find that side by side with the literary language, Sanskrit, there existed what is called by "Panini", the famous Grammarian, the "Basha" or the language of the people, which is only a variety of Sanskrit and not a separate dialect. The Aryan colonists of early days, including the Brahmins, did not preserve themselves from contamination. As the non-Aryans and the Aryans began freely to make use of the language called the "Basha", the current of corruption set in with full vigour and there grew up gradually new dialects called "Prakrits", which are varieties of Sanskrit and Bashas, mingled with non-Aryan language or languages.

TELUGU A VIKRUTI.

But we have stated that Telugu is a vikruti, a term which means literally "change". Though the lexicon of Prakrits is enriched with non-Aryan words, the Prakrits are fundamentally Aryan ; on the other hand though about two-thirds of the vocabulary of the Andhra language were borrowed directly from Sanskrit, and indirectly from Prakrits, just as English from Latin and French, its grammar is non-Sanskrit, like English whose grammar is Anglo-Saxon and not Latin. Just as English is placed among the Gothic and not among the Roman languages, Telugu is placed among the non-Aryan languages.

Thus, Telugu or Thenugu, as its name "Vikruti" implies, is a mutation of the ancient Andhra tongue by the admixture of Sanskrit and Prakrits and possibly also of some words of Kolarian or Turanian origin.

The language thus formed is of course a compound and complex one and as such it must needs be irregular and consequently difficult for study. This disadvantage is more than counterbalanced by the advantages that the Telugu language possesses. As stated already Telugu is a sweet language and as such styled as the " Sweet Italian of the East " or the language flowing with honey, as the Telugu pandits are proud to say of their language.

Secondly as a compound language Telugu is certainly rich both in the number and variety of words.

Lastly Telugu, which was once

entirely agglutinative, for now nearly 60 per cent. of the words used in it is Sanskrit, can be called to a great extent an inflexional language, like all Sanskritic dialects or languages. The languages of the world are divided according to the geneological or genetical order into "Aryan," "Semitic," "Hamatic," "Scythian," "Maleo-polynesian" and "American." According to another classification known as "Morphological" all the languages of the world are distinguished as "inflexional," "agglutinative" or "monosyllabic."

Telugu as well as Tamil are of Scythian origin according to the first division and in the order of second classification Telugu, unlike

Tamil, has now become to a great extent inflexional in character.

TELUGU AND THE EARLY ANDHRA KINGS.

The early Andhra kings did not at all encourage their mother tongue and it received only a step-motherly treatment in their hands.

It was considered as the language of the common people like the "Basha" of their Aryan neighbours. Just as Norman French was the language of the court in England after the Norman conquest, so also the Andhra kings and nobles began to use Sanskrit as the most polished of languages then, as it is now, which is borne out by the fact that Sanskrit means "all perfect." On the other hand the Andhra kings encouraged Sanskrit in all possible ways. "The Andhra supremacy", says R.C. Dutt, "over Northern India marks a stage in the development of Indian literature. Centuries before the advent of Christ, the Andhras rose to be a great civilised power in the Deccan and started schools of science and learning." The Andhra rulers were great munificent patrons of learning and their royal patronage was freely extended upon the pundits of the time. Besides they themselves were authors of several Sanskrit books.

They invited all the learned men of India and rewarded them

according to their merits and one among those so rewarded was "Kalidasa," the most famous of Indian Poets.

THE NEW TERM "ANDHRO-DRAVIDA."

Tamil is no doubt an independent language. Telugu though also an independent one was considered originally by mistake as of Aryan origin, owing to her free admixture with Sanskrit and its dialects. The missionaries of South India steadily mastered Tamil and its kindred languages and finding them to be cognate brought them under one group and called them "Dravidian." It was only after this group had been formed that the missionaries began to work in the northern districts where Telugu was spoken and thus the language of the Andhras was not considered, when the Dravidian grouping took place. When, in course of time, the term Dravidian was acknowledged by scholars as a philological expression, Telugu was looked upon merely as a dialect of Sanskrit.

But a closer and deeper study and examination of the language, the Vedas and the non-Aryan traces of the Andhras disclosed the mistake and the scholars not knowing what to do in this dilemma conveniently brought Telugu under the Dravidian group.

This, we venture to think, is a great mistake, because those that are responsible for this classification betray their gross ignorance of the ancient glorious history of the Andhras, their origin and independent growth. So the term Dravidian should be applied only to the Tamils and their neighbours on the west coast and not to the Telugus.

Not to comfound the terms "Dravidian" and "Andhra" and mix up Telugu with Tamil, we would suggest that the term "Andhro-Dravida," should be acknowledged by scholars as a common philological designation for all the languages of southern India.

This term "Andhro-Dravida", it is well to mention, is not altcgether a new one, for it was already used in the 7th century A.D. by no less a person than "Kumarilla Batta," a controversial writer of great eminence.

It will not be considered unreasonable, if we go a step further and suggest that the term "Dravida" may be replaced by the term "Andhra," to designate all the languages of Southern India.

For on the authority of the "Indian Wisdom" one can affirm that the Tamils were once living in the Punjab, speaking the same old Andhra tongue and completely identifying themselves with the

Andhras of our day. But the term Dravidian, as we have already pointed out, with all its significance can rightly be applied to Tamil and its allied language Malayalam, for the etymological identity of Kerala, the land of the Malayalees and Chera, is recognised by philologists of high authority. Further in early times the kingdom of Chera included that of Kerala. We may now consider whether the Kanarese, another important section of the people of Southern India and their language can be classed as Andhra or Dravidian.

IS KANARESE AN ANDHRA TONGUE?

According to Monier Williams the Andhras and the Dravidas, must have had the same cradle, like the Aryans, somewhere in the regions of Central Asia between the Oxus and Jaxartes and forced their way into India settling at first, on the banks of the Indus, and at a very early period, the latter leaving the former, must have occupied their present home in the south.

History holds no record of the existence of the Kanarese nation, in the early times, for the simple reason, that they had no kingdom of their own, nor is it mentioned anywhere that they were included in the list of northern peoples, or kingdoms. History tells us that in the first century before Christ, during the reign of Krishna of Andhra dynasty, the town of Nasik, near the source of the Godavari on the Western Ghats, was included in the Andhra dominions which thus stretched across India, from the Bay of Bengal to the Arabian Sea. In the year 27 B.C. the Kanva King who was the lord of all the North including the famous kingdom of "Magada", was slain by the Andhras and his vast kingdom was annexed to the extensive regions that were already under their control. The mighty kingdom of Magada, which Alexander the

Great, failed to conquer owing to dissensions among his soldiers, was in time conquered by the Andhras.

AT ONE TIME ANDHRAS RULED ENTIRE INDIA.

In addition to this, Southern India also, (to point out that Southern India also was at one time ruled by the Andhras) must have been brought, under the mighty Andhra sway, as is seen, from the inscription found, in the 19th of the 24 caves, fashioned by the great monk Sramana, at Nasik in the reign of the Andhra king "Krishna Satakarni" who is described therein, as one "whose army drank the waters of the three oceans."

Mr. A. J. Saldanna, in his book, on Kcnkani castes, says that the Konkan was ruled by the Andhras from about 100 B.C. to about 400 A.D. It was only from the beginning of the 5th century A.D. that the Kadambas and after some breaks the Ballalas, both, Kanarese by race, began to rule. This will coincide with the fall of the Andhra power. In the 5th century A.D., the Andhras who had lost the kingdom of Magada in the north, were forced to give up also the country along the western coast, which from that time was ruled by the Kadambas. During the long ruie of the Andhras there must have been free intercourse between the rulers and the ruled and so there is considerable truth in the statement of Monier Williams, that the Kanarese resemble the Telugus, rather than the Tamils. From the foregoing may we not reasonably conclude that the Kanarese should be brought under Andhra and not under Dravidian?

Further that the people now known as Kanarese must have been a section of the old Andhras and it is very probable that the country on the western coast separated itself from the main Andhra nation or kingdom, in the beginning of the 5th century A.D. and that it was only then that it formed an independent kingdom under the rule of Kadambas. This may be considered as the beginning of the Kanarese nation.

THE TERMS OF "VADUGU" AND "ARAVAMU".

The bulk of the people however, among the Telugus and the Tamils, do not use the philological names of their respective languages. The Telugus call their Tamil brethren "Arava" and their language "Aravamu", while the Tamils use the word "Vadugu" for the Telugu language and "Vadugar" for the Telugus.

The Tamil word for the north is "Vadakku" and the Telugus who live in the North are therefore called "Vadugar" and their language Vadugu, the language of the people who live in the north. But with regard to the term "Aravamu", it is difficult to say what it exactly signifies. We may attempt a plausible explanation (which is also held by many Telugu Pandits), but we may not vouch for its correctness. Splitting the word into a-not, and ravam=sound, we can say that the term has the meaning of unsounding or not musical, which is, of course, used by the Telugus, in contradistinction with Telugu which is the most musical of all Indian languages. Both these words are, however, contemptuous terms.

ANDHRAS RULED INDIA FOR OVER 400 YEARS.

Finally not speculating like the ancient Hindus that "Jambudvipa" was encircled by the seven great oceans of Butter, Milk, Curds, Ghee and Sugarcane juice, etc., but only making a free use of the helpful telescope of history, we learn the signal origin and the wonderful and independent growth of the mysterious Andhra nation, who ruled over a vast tract of land, for more than 400 years, a period unusually long in the history of any nation in the world. We have said that the word "Andhra" also means "invincible" and it well applies to them, for they were a great military power, who ruled the whole of India, at one time, including the mighty kingdom of Magada and also, Southern India, who saved Hindustan, from the clutches of foreign invaders, Yavanas, Pallavas, and chiefly from the fangs of the dreadful Sakas, who inflamed by the glowing reports of the wealth and magnificence of Pataliputra the Indian Babylon, which excelled its Assyrian rival, in wealth and power, poured in, in vast hordes, on its fruitful soil, as is well proved by the long and eloquent inscription recorded in 144 A.D. by a famous Andhra queen of the time.

THE GREAT MILITARY POWER OF THE ANDHRAS.

With the aid of history, therefore, we are able to say that the Andhras grew up gradually and in course of time became one of the most powerful nations, if we include the Aryan rulers and excluding them, certainly, the most powerful, that ever ruled "the Pride of the Orient" as this vast Indian Empire is sometimes called. Alexander the Great, the foremost of heroes, acknowledged as the conqueror of the world, since ambition was still his predominant passion, resolved to invade India and conquer it.

Nothing was an obstacle to him.

Victory followed victory. He crossed the river Indus. The mighty kingdom of "Magada", lay in front of him, "could he advance hither and plant his standard, all Hindustan would be at his feet". No, he could not, or at least he did not. In course of time, to the gratification of every Andhra, on the same battlements which refused access to the Macedonian standard, the invincible Andhra flag was flying gaily. There were, and are still, nations that have made great conquests. But with only a few, the conquered were contented. Lend your ears to the eloquent testimony of the imperishable rocks at "Karli" and "Nasik."

The Andhra empire was ruled by kings " who levied and expended the taxes according to the sacred law ". Again the words of the second inscription mentioned above, " whose face was as the sun kissed lotus ", clearly show the mutual love between the rulers and the ruled.

THE KINGDOM OF VIJAYANAGAR.

The mighty Aryo-Andhra kingdom of Magada, and also the very Andhra kingdom itself fell, and in time, Vijayanagar the city of victory, a new Telugu kingdom, rose to prominence. History tells us that its capital city was 24 miles in circumference.

The army put forth in battle by the king of Vijayanagar, against the Sultan's troops, exceeded that of the Japanese, in the late war, against the Russians, showing thereby how powerful the Andhras were, even after their downfall in Northern India. Vijayanagar, known as " Humpi " or the forgotten empire, was also named as Vidyanagar, because the Telugus esteemed and encouraged learning very much and thus added more lustre to their past glory. Its kings were great patrons of literature and arts and some of them were good poets themselves. In the Court of the great Krishnadeva of Vijayanagar, there were eight celebrated poets known as "Ashtadigajamulu," or the elephants of the eight corners of the world.

THE TELUGUS AT MADURA.

In this connection it will not be fair, on our part, if we fail to say a few words about the Telugus of Madura. Some of the letters of St. Francis Xavier are full of the Telugus who carried fire and sword to the south, and were a source of terror to the people there.

Among the kings of Madura, who has not heard of Thirumal Naidu? His famous palace and temple at Madura are even to-day objects of great admiration and wonder and attract many visitors even from foreign countries.

Southern India was too small for these kings, for one among these kings, named Sreevijayasinha and his two successors, ruled also "Lanka," Ceylon, known to the ancient Greeks, as "Mahagrammah."

CONCLUSION.

This is in short the Origin and the Glorious Past of the Andhras and what wonder then, that there exists an eloquent Tamil proverb, which is, "can there be any betterment than that of the Telugus"?

The demand of such a nation *for a separate* province and university on a linguistic *basis, is,* we think, quite reasonable and proper.